Start a Business

How to Work from Home And Make Money Blogging

T. Whitmore

Copyright © 2016 by T. Whitmore All Right Reserved.

No part of this publication may be reproduced, distributed, or transmitted in any form or by any means, including photocopying, recording, or other electronic or mechanical methods, or by any information storage and retrieval system without the prior written permission of the publisher, except in the case of very brief quotations embodied in critical reviews and certain other noncommercial uses permitted by copyright law.

Table of Contents

Introduction

What is Blogging?

Picking a Niche

Choosing a Proper Platform

Focusing Fully on Content

Meeting and Socializing with other Bloggers

Write for other Bloggers

Analyzing Data

Monetizing Your Site

Maintaining Your Blog

SEO

Hone Your Creativity

Strategize Your Marketing Efforts

Rinse and Repeat

Staying in the Know

Keep Your Head above Water

Never Give up Blogging

Your FREE Gift

Introduction:

Our internet growth over the last couple of decades has caused an almighty expansion! An expansion of unlimited opportunities for individuals and private organizations all around to make lots and lots of money all over the entire globe! The world is full of myriads of competition every corner that you turn, especially online. And especially in the blogging world. When we begin to look inside of ourselves, and we mentally and intelligently think outside of the box, we can then think of alternative ways that we can make extra money. We should not concentrate on the traditional way of making money, as traditional ways take too long. Traditional ways, cut individuals off with a salary that remains somewhat stagnant and only increases minimally over the years. In this book,

Making Money From Blogging, we will be looking and thinking outside of the box, because this strategy enables individuals great successes and begins to open doors that lead into unlimited opportunities, rather than the traditional way of making money; the old nine to five.

Thinking outside of the box when it comes to making money is the only way an individual can exit a stagnant salary and leave the rat race. Billionaires and millionaires all around the globe have stated that they have taken many risks, to lead them to their fortunes. As a blogger, a career blogger, we need to be able to determine good risks and bad risks. Every business owner should definitely analyze this strategy. Also, make sure that you have a safety net of income in your bank account before you begin your blogging career full-time. Otherwise you may be eating ramen day in and day out, for pennies on the dollar. If you have a family to tend to, do not start a blogger career with zero income!

Make wise decisions, each business entrepreneur needs not only a safety net, but needs start-up costs; so before you dart at your competition, make sure that you set-up the logistics with your finances before you begin. Usually six months' worth of income is ideal, just in case you need to buy yourself time on your monthly bills. As a blogger, you don't need to be an artist who suffers financially, if you prepare yourself the right way, you can succeed with reasonable effort. But let us warn you now; succeeding in blogging requires strategically planning your finances like a game of   before you begin. Later, the money will follow you, all while you provide blogging content from the bottom of your heart. People love blogs that pour out their souls. Not in an annoying way, but an artistic type of way. If you love a topic, that's how you will come across through your online writing diction. Communication is everything in the world of blogging, learn communication strategies, and delve into the world of independent blogging.

    Yes, every one of us likes money, not because we want to like it, but because we have to like it. Money moves our entire globe on a daily basis. The world works with: services, commodities, and exchanges. Of course we'd better love money, if we don't want to end up poor and on the streets and without any food. But keep in mind, this isn't always the case, as everyone needs to know that money does not create eternal happiness. We should know that relationships and experiences are really what create an ultimate meaning and belonging to human lives all around. So if your immediate goal when you start blogging is a lot of money, get out of here! Every human wants to feel accepted and wants to feel some sort of unity. Blogging can give us a sense of belonging and unity, blogging can help others as well. Blogging can help us vent. Inside of this book, *Making Money from Blogging,* you will discover chock-full information about the steps anyone can take, if you want to get serious about making money and blogging.

Yes, people blog for a full-time job now, twenty years ago, a grandmother complained about how her granddaughter was wasting her life away on her computer; twenty years later, the granddaughter is a multi-millionaire, being that she created an online app. Our guess is, the grandmother is shocked with her granddaughter's computer successes. The internet helps us individuals become limitless with the work we can produce. Are you a content genius and do you want to start seeing green dough roll inside of your bank account? Open this book if you are willing to take a moment, learn, and implement, the helpful blogging strategies inside, will be worth the knowledge. This book, *Making Money from Blogging,* was sent to you by chance, go ahead and enhance your lives and delve into this book. Watch what will unfold, we're already sold on our advice strategies.

Inside, Learn Various Blogging Method's to Make Real Money!

- Don't only learn the basics about blogging, learn the in's-and-the-out's
- Learn to provide help for each and every one of your visitors
- Provide quality blog posts, otherwise, risk your audience.
- Learn to construct a clean and sophisticated stylistic blog, and learn how to market, analyze, and monetize your blog appropriately
- Learn about yourself and your internal wants and desires
- Learn about what you don't want
- Utilize the strategies inside so that way you can provide you and your family with long-term

financial freedom. Every hard working family deserves freedom, and every blogger is grateful for their own freedom to create

- Make life better, all around, blog
- Communicate

Open this book, *Making Money from Blogging,* if you are serious about learning blogging strategies and techniques, and if you are serious about making real hard cash from your niche loving passion. Heed this advice, this is no easy task, it takes, gaining a groove and momentum, through practice, trial, and error. By learning more information, we are automatically enabling ourselves for greater things in life as bloggers. Think about it, if you learn to blog well enough, you might be able to situate your life, so you can solely work from the comfort of your own home, hence avoiding all of the world catastrophes that exist in the year 2016.

We want to help you, the blogger, get to a point where you can sit in the comfort of your pajamas, if you so choose to and work. This doesn't mean that you can be lazy at your own home; otherwise absolutely no money will be flying into your bank account. Set-up a proper office environment, this is an absolute must. Make sure your office is comfortable to work in, safe, and free of external distractions. After all, you want to get serious about starting your own blog, so let's get serious and let's start to think about your blogging career as a business, because once this business starts bringing in any kind of income, then it is darn right Uncle Sam will want a piece of your financial gains.

Yes, good old taxes! A nice office set-up, a fast internet connection, a phone, skills, willingness to learn, drive, writing and editing skills, an eye for design, and a fast working computer are all necessary components in order to get started blogging. If you have no idea about the previous components necessary to start a blog, then before you enter, brush up on your skills, as design, computer, and content skills are a must, these skills are relevant to starting a new blog. If you can't afford University training or a seminar or workshop at the moment, then the internet is a good start, as it provides a plethora of information regarding design, technical computer skills, sales, and writing advice. Brush up on each individual skill, if you need to. Continue to read if you want to learn how to start *Making Money from Blogging*. Nope, it is not a walk in the park, blogging is hard thought, so get ready to work, but in this case, you will be working and building for yourself, not a corporation. Remember, what you bring in, is all up to you.

What is Blogging?

Blogging is a new edge way to express oneself through multimedia. Blogging used to be more for content only, but as the years have advanced, and computers became more intelligent, creators all around continued to excel with their ideas. Blog's have become a conglomeration of text, photos, videos, etc. All of these forms of art can be mixed together to create a new type of media, coining the term new media arts. Blogging is a place where we can explore ourselves, our minds, and our deepest desires. Through writing and ultimate creation, we are able to experience and feel. We are also able to alleviate any stress that we may be having when we create. If you are looking to make money off of your blog, you'd better choose a topic that doesn't bore you, otherwise it is possible that you will write and post drab content, which will affect your blog in the long-run. No one wants that. You need to choose a topic that uplifts you! A topic you are incredibly excited about so your love shines through computer screens all around!

How Has Blogging Advanced?

Blogging in today's day and age has advanced because individuals all over the globe, now have access to the internet, providing a platform where individuals can explore their skills, create a killer blog, and succeed their way to their own bank account compilation. It sure is possible to succeed from blogging alone. The only blogger's who make real money have a bit of genius and hustle inside of them. Blogging has been able to unite a globe; it has also been known to spread propaganda and ill intent. Use blogging wisely in the year 2016. The access is there, formal education is not a necessity, but sure it helps. Blogging has advanced because in the year 2016 blogging has become sort of a trend, we see blogs constantly come and go on a consistent basis. This then leads us to question ourselves and our own blogs; we can start to ask ourselves certain questions like, "How can I make my blog stand out from the myriads of blogs that are currently online?" Questions like this before you begin are absolute imperative to your blogging business. If you don't ask yourself these direct questions, than it is highly possible your strategy will be all over the place, causing you to lack in quality via your precious money-maker, your blog.

Blogging Timeline

Of course curiosity is the best intent an individual can have in life, especially when it comes to learning about new skills and new ways to earn more income for your family and for yourself. Blogging started when the advent of the internet hit in the early nineties, a man by the name of Tim Berners-Lee coined the term, 'world wide web,' according to Wikipedia. We are now in the year 2016 and the birth of the internet is still fresh, it's still vibrant as ever! Blogging has never been so useful. People read all of the time and if they are reading and buying your blog services, products, memorabilia, whatever it is that you sell, well then you have tapped a market and you 'd better keep tapping, before someone else taps before you. Keep in mind, the more creative you are, the more income you will turn in. Smartphones, everyone has one in the year 2016! Even the ten year old kid down the street, they have a smartphone too! Plus ipads, iwatches, these technological gadgets are huge! This is such a huge market, so perhaps you are a writer for children's online ebooks? Well, as long as your illustrations look rad, and your content is cool, chances are the kid will want your book! Add your eBooks on your blog posts and on your blog site homepage don't forget to customize your categories and tags, as this will make it more helpful for online seekers to find you through a keyword search on Google. Sooner or later, parents will be knocking at your online blogging website looking to buy your cool and entertaining content. Use your skills! Don't ever forget how important it is to have a sense of visualization style. Remember, if your blogging page looks choppy, unedited, and the photos are grainy, yet unattractive, or unacceptable, you will lose an audience as quick as you posted all of that junk! So we wise, and hold class and professional poise!

What Determines A Successful Blog?

Since this particular book is about, *'How to Make Money Blogging,'* we can plan to measures successes by analytics and revenue brought in. Having a successful blog takes time; it can take several years, if you are not already a full-time blogger. Some blogs hit big right away, while other blogs diminish into the vast black space of the internet deep depths, never receiving any visitors. You never want to fall into a box where you don't receive any visitors. The whole point of a blog is to share content and gain the respect and the trust of your readers. Having a successful blog means that your mind and your soul are in unison, because you are actually creating and presenting topics and subjects about things you love. A successful blogs rakes in a lot of visitors, fulfills your soul, relieves your stress, honors your creativity, and brings in income.

Picking a Niche

Picking a niche is a hard task to do, especially if you have no idea what you are interested in, if you are in this boat, than soul searching to find out what you are interested in, is your best bet. In order to help you choose the niche that you want to blog about, you need to think about something that you love. Do you love to hike and explore the world? If this is so, than you might think about creating a travel blog. Are you a seasoned karate instructor? There is a lot more than you can do with this side skill than just teach classes at a karate school. Here, think outside the box, if you are in fact a karate instructor, you could write content about your experiences, you could sell eBooks on your website, perhaps you can create ten eBooks, imagine you sell over a million copies at $2.99 a piece? At this point, if you do reach this point, you will be venturing into million dollar status! Let's see, as a karate teacher, you could also offer online video classes to distant students. But before you do this, make sure to get good reviews from your former clients so that way your online community and the online world will have a sense of trust, when it comes to selling your particular brand, online buyers need a sense of trust established. Buyers have choices, and as a blogger, an entrepreneur, you always want to cater to your viewers more than your competitors.

Questions to ask yourself:
- What do I love to do in my free time?
- What interests me?
- What kinds of external and internal desires do I have?

- What do I enjoy researching?
- Simply put, is there anything particular that you are interested in?
- What do you like to read?
- What kind of content do you prefer to write?
- What kind of images do you like to see?

Choose a niche that solves your hearts woes, and begin to create your blog. Make sure to also plan out your blog posts. Next, plan an opening marketing strategy, target friends and family in their email, and target acquaintances or coworkers through social media. Let everyone know about the niche and blog you have chosen, this is a perfect time to get people interested in your blog. But before you launch anything, make sure that your launch has an utmost professional appearance. You will want to think of launch marketing strategies.

Blog Launch Marketing Strategies Include:

- Create a Facebook page that connects to your blog
- Create a nice email flyer on Illustrator or Photoshop
- Email family and friends
- Invite family and friends to your Facebook page, mention a link to your blog
- Connect your blog posts to your social media sites, every time you post on your blog, you will be able to spread the same post on to your connected social media sites

- Make sure your images pop with clarity and your content is error-free
- Pay Facebook and buy ad time, people will then hear about the launch of your blogging site while they browse on Facebook.
- You can also buy paid advertising on Twitter
- If you don't have a budget to work with, make daily posts and daily shares, this marketing method won't hurt, remember to reel in quality visitors only

Choosing a Proper Platform

Now let's drift our minds from niches to platforms. If you want to make some real money, this is the first and foremost step that you must take; retrieving a platform that allows you to manage all of your content. Decide to choose domains that allow you to monetize. Now, if you are utterly new to this, a domain is a .com. You want to be able to control the visitors and the incoming finances that are soon to be raking in. Don't opt to choose a free website, as you will limit the amount of capabilities you will have, choose to use a domain owned by you, you'll have much more abilities and capabilities as the administrator. There are websites such as fatcow.com which offer cheap prices to buy dot.coms, sometimes the start-up cost won't topple $100.00 for a whole entire year, that's doable. You are the blogger, the entrepreneur, don't let the third party website preparer take your advertising money, don't let third party corporations stunt your blogging growth, you are better than that. Of course, starting a blog isn't always free, but we recommend using Blogger (it's free), it's connected to the large IT player Google and Google Ads. Wordpress is good too, but in order to fully cap on full capabilities you'll need to pay an annual fee, the cost is under $500.00 U.S.D., and affordable. Although, if Blogger offers a free platform and you are struggling to start your blog, then free is a terrific option, choose Blogger. Blogger is more user friendly than Wordpress, but if you want to grow your blog in the future, you as a blogger will soon need to know the full technicality when it comes to Wordpress. WordPress is used by corporations and individuals all around and has built a good reputation over the years in the blogging world. Companies like The Huffington Post and Tech Crunch started the whole blogging trend, and now they are multi-millionaire companies! Just think of the indention that you as a blogger can make on society. Yes you can make a difference, but remember you must certainly blog with poise, noise, and keep it consistent. There are many platforms out there, just like there are many products out there on the market, every product and service claims they do all sorts of wonders, it's a selling tact. Always research the software that you will be downloading, or the service in which you will be using, and try to stick with the bigger name brand platforms, as there will be more credibility, reliability, and security that will be delivered to you and your blogging needs.

Trial and Error

If we want to succeed at anything in life we all have to fail at something in order to understand our past mistakes. In life, if we don't know something, chances are we might fail the first time, but if we do our very best to learn from the mistake and no longer implement the failed attempt strategy than we are bettering ourselves for future growth and advancement. Some of you are dealing with this circumstance, you started a blog, you post and then you get no feedback, no viewers, no nothing. Zilch, absolutely nothing! You have tried your hardest, but you just didn't seem to tap the right algorithm to allow you to become visible online. Stop experiencing error. How? By thinking through your strategies and by trying to make the best sound and logical decisions that you possibly can. If you are serious about making money from a blog, than it is highly advised that you start treating this like a responsible business. Before you begin full force, start accepting the challenges that you most likely will face. Always be positive about your new endeavor, *Making Money from Blogging,* and keep in mind that you are going to have to spend a lot of your own free time building your own blog if you want it to actually work. Glory doesn't come from being lazy. In order to succeed at *Making Money from Blogging,* you need to whip yourself into shape and you need to create, create, create! Now we will be absolutely clear about this particular piece of advice, creating just anything will absolutely not work! When you are writing, you need to make sure that you are creating content that matters! Content that has myriads of errors and that has very little thought will be found out sooner or later, so do yourself a favor and only create the very best, your very best! Remember, prestige will gain you higher rewards in the long-term, so please keep this in mind when learning how to *Make Money From Blogging*.

Focusing Fully On Content

Before you even begin to focus on blogging you need to make sure that you are focusing on creating quality content, otherwise you may risk losing a reader quickly and most certainly, if your content or visual images, or even advertisements, offend or bombard your viewers too much they might not ever visit your blog site again, now that would be an utter devastation! When we speak about quality content, we want to make sure that the content is error proof. But how do we go about knowing if it is error proof? The answer is easy and if you don't know it, than you might need to brush up on your skills. Simple, edit your work rigorously! Or have someone else edit your work for you, but keep in mind, eventually the editor will want to be paid. Hone, practice, and improve your editing skills. People all over the world will be reading your content and blog that you published, so keep it fresh, keep it clean in grammar, punctuation, and spelling. Every reader and viewer prefers a smooth and flowing type of read and a crisp image. By now, you should have already chosen your particular niche that you will concentrate on, so you can now focus on creating a lot of content, and by a lot, we mean, this is a consistent task that needs to be done on the daily. Plan out your publishing and posting schedule.

Set times and dates for yourself if you need to, in fact we highly recommend this strategy in order to keep you completely organized and on schedule. If you are not at the point where you can quit your day job just yet, than it is wise that you set aside certain times and days that you can write and concentrate on your blog. Creating an itinerary when it comes to strategizing your blogs success is most ideal. Even if you can only set aside two hours a night or two hours a week, you can make great progress on your blog. Make sure the content that you produce is pure quality content, we will keep mentioning this fact throughout our book, as it will throw any reader off, if your content is not up to par.

If you happen to be a poet, make sure that you have quality poetry, don't just slop just anything together, always put your best foot forward. If one blog idea doesn't work, learn to chalk it up, and move to another blog idea, don't just give up on your blog because it didn't work the first time. Make sure to practice and perfect your skills, otherwise your blog will remain stagnant, and what is a stagnant blog on the internet? A waste of space! Well those words are a little too harsh, so we take it back. We know, you worked hard on your blog thus far, so keep it up, but absolutely do not forget to market your blog on social media appropriately and affectivity. Otherwise there is a chance you could become invisible, as the masses will overshadow your glorious words waiting to be read. There are companies that started as blogs, Tech Crunch, and The Huffington Post, are a couple of examples. You should aspire to be like these companies, they are informative, highly followed, and now multi-millionaires. We are not necessarily saying to write in their particular niche or tone, but it may be wise to take a look at their sites, and recognize, when it comes to blogging, if you are good, consistent, well-liked, a good marketer, a good seller, and the list goes on, then you could in fact make it big like The Huffington Post or Tech Crunch!

Meeting and Socializing With Other Bloggers

If you don't take time away from content producing and designing, then it is possible that you will set yourself up for failure. When you socialize on platforms that support other bloggers, it allows you the blogger to become more visible. Socializing and interacting with other bloggers allows bloggers all around to relate, unite, and come together and discuss. Discussion is important as the content will remain online and socializing will be sure to help you and blog get noticed. Get out there and socialize on your various blog websites, otherwise your blog could possibly suffer alienation. Being anti-social in the blogging world never gets anyone anywhere. Bloggers and creators always need other collaborators. Gain a good online reputation by providing quality work, ask to write on other blogs, and make sure that you always knock on doors, well, emails in this case. If you are writing with a journalistic approach, always back up your statements if resources are needed, otherwise you'll lose your journalistic credibility with readers. Always cite and link when appropriate, this can't be stressed enough. Never forget to cite your sources and quotations, this is an absolute imperative! Edit, edit, edit, all posts otherwise suffer being judged and thrown out!

The online market can be a cruel world, individuals all around do not see how quickly the internet is evolving, hence, why some individuals aren't selective when it comes to their online posts, don't be that person, and only post relevant information, that you strongly believe in, as the results will reap more rewards and get more reviews, comments, and insight. Controversy online works too for bloggers to gain in the ranks and views, but remember how populated our very own online system is, don't forget it is a dark-filled land of propaganda!

Be Sure To Download The WordPress Application on Your Smartphone

Since smartphones these days are so accessible to individuals all around, we recommend that you download the WordPress application. Downloading this application will help you keep up with blog posts on-the-go. Everyone has busy schedules, so what better way to keep up with your viewers and commentaries than with an application at hand! You can choose to be notified every time someone comments, pings back, or likes your posts; this will make it easier to connect with other bloggers and people simply looking to read. Connect at all times of the day and post whenever you feel like it! Of course, since we only recommend you post pure quality, if you are on-the-go and you don't have a pen, certainly jot down your idea in this application, but make sure to save your post as a draft, then later, when you have some quiet time to yourself, make sure that you go over your words, your images, your categories, and your tags, before finalizing the content that you will be publishing. Having the ability to manage your content and your social sites at the palm of your hand will keep you not only up-to-date, but it will keep you tuned in via real-time. This method will make sure that you are ready for the world of blogging. In fact, we recommend that you download all of the applications that you are currently using for your blog, download them on your smartphone, this will make sure that you can keep up with everything, including rapid random thoughts, social connections, and other bloggers.

Write For Other Bloggers

 So we understand, you are not quite yet to the point of owning your own blogging business just yet, but you do have a blog that is established with daily followers, you have a nice portfolio, and a professional and clean looking template, so now is your time to reach out to other bloggers. Go online, research, and discover new and interesting blogs. Determine what kind of content and visualizations interest you. What do you like to look at? Determine who your competitors are and find niches that are similar to yours. Intently study.

Find more established links and write to the blog owner, but before you do, make sure that you grasp the tone of the actual blog before sending any pitches to the blog owner. Remember that first opinions are everything, these other bloggers, will only meet you online once, so you might as well make sure that you put your best blog foot forward, otherwise risk getting shunned early on in the game of online blogging. No one wants to be shunned, otherwise it will be harder to become visible online. Don't let your blog die out too early.

Keep in mind to always be nice and encouraging to other bloggers, they deal with the same obstacles that you have dealt with too, of course each blogger is always at a different stage in his or her career, after all it depends on the individual and their independent drive and motivation. You are the ultimate blogger, keep telling yourself that. Once you finally make online friends with popular and established bloggers, apply to posts on their blog, make sure you professionally contact them through their blog's contact page, and make sure you set up a pitch and an idea that actually has relevance to their page. Once you do this, send your pitch with poise, attach samples of work, links, and your biography, plus absolutely do not forget to add a contact email and phone number for the blogger to contact you back. Make it easy for them to find and browse your past work. Keyword, visibility.

Okay, finally another blogger recognizes your content and visualization skills, and invites you to guest blog on their page. Should you do it? The answer is easy, of course you should. The reasons? There are plenty of reasons. One, your writing will be seen, you might not get paid the first time when you get accepted to guest blog, but what will occur is that you will you become more visible, especially if you are guest blogging on a well-established blog that many people follow and read on a daily basis. So if you have an opportunity to guest blog, you'd better start blogging, as the more traffic that is linked to your blog, ultimately means more followers for your blog in the future.

Blogging takes time, and it takes time to gain traffic. If people don't have a clue about you, how do you think they will make it to your blog in the first place? You only have one chance when it comes to making a positive appearance on a guest blog, people judge quickly, so give them your raw soul, your love, your cold-blooded passion. Blogging is meant to be an internal release for some, enjoy what you do, help others, and share the love.

Analyzing Data, Visitors, etc.

When first deciding on your blog platform you need to be sure that you have a blogging platform that allows you to monetize your web earnings, if you don't do this in the beginning of your blog, than you could possibly lose out. We can't mention this enough, don't open a blogging account where the third party website limits your blogging abilities. We said this before, and we are going to say it again, as we see far too many good bloggers become tangled in this kind of web, their followers are enormous, but they are on a third party website, so the blogger ends up not getting paid for his or her marketing efforts on the ad side. Choose a site like Blogger, pay the premium for WordPress, or buy your own domain and map it to WordPress, but don't use a third party that doesn't allow you to monetize your earnings! Read the fine print before you agree and start publishing your content. There are many routes you can take, but never fall into the trap where you can't make money off of GoogleAd Words, or off of advertising in general. Some sites block monetizing, you as a new blogger, need to be aware of this fact. Don't fall into this scam and trap, we are warning you now!

When you are finally able to analyze the incoming traffic to your blog's site, you can start utilizing newly learned knowledge about the people who are following your blog, once you find useful information, make sure to cater to your visitor's needs.

Let us get one fact straight, in the world of blogging, traffic and visitors are the blood of blogging. If traffic doesn't run through the bloggers pages and veins then there would be no heart beating blog, your blog would simply be dead. Keep your visitors satiated at all times! Once you are able to learn the art of this, money will be running in, whether you like it or not.

Monetizing Your Site

Now this is the whole entire reason as to why we are reading this particular book, now let's get into the nuts and bolts about, *Making Money from Blogging,* Ah what is monetizing? If you don't know about monetizing than get out of here and stop reading this now! No, in all seriousness, this is why we are here, monetizing is why we are here. We are here of course because we want to have the ability to work on our own time, and to have access and freedom to uncapped monetary gains, that is why we are here in the first place.

Ways To Monetize Your Blog Include (Short Version):

- Advertising (Google Adwords & Adsense)

- Amazon (affiliate marketing)
- EBooks
- Webinars (paid) Online Classes
- Services
- Advertisements, Private Companies
- Products
- Videos
- Audio
- Content

Adding EBooks, Products, and Services to Your Blog

You can add ads onto your blog page and let your blog complacently sit online, of course that would be a complete newbie approach, don't do that! An entrepreneur who usually succeeds always diversifies their portfolio, and you know what this causes? This causes an influx of more streams of income. EBooks these days sell! There are notable online EBook sellers that have been known to hit it big and sell millions of copies, all from solely advertising online, eBooks have become a trend.

EBooks have changed the way that we read, of course, this is because of the edge and growth technology has seen, but because of this fact, we can now begin to realize how many paths there are, when it comes to seeking out different ways to make money online! Adding other products onto your blogging site, after your readers trust you (of course), is ideal, because not only will this allow you to gain income, it will allow you to continue your business. Incoming money will keep your blogging business thriving. Always be weary upon what you directly advocate for. If it doesn't feel right, it's probably not.

Connect To All External Links

Connecting your blog to an external link should be implemented because the more links that you direct to your blog, the higher rating your traffic will be. And let's get this straight, in the blogging world, traffic really is everything. Advertising is also a big revenue source when it comes to blogging so link, link, link, and don't you start to think twice.

Using Ads and Videos

Using ads and videos will make sure that you are gaining viewers. People, well, the masses anyway, the masses love images! You always want to capture your readers with interesting imagery as this will immediately catch their attention, catching the attention of the masses will put your blog on the forefront.

If you do use videos, we always highly suggest that you use YouTube, or some kind of video platform system that actually lets you monetize your earnings through viewers watched and ads played. Using eye catching media will be sure to catch your audience in a glimpse of a second. Snap! But also we aware, that initial glance appearance is your first objective. You want to basically position yourself at a stance where not only is your content visually intriguing, but your content is complete quality, also your headline has to be a clickable attention-getter! If no one understands what you will be talking about in your blog post, than why would they be interested, when it comes to reading your content in the first place? That just is not happening! Impress your readers with lively content!

Gain Quality Audience, Rather Than Quantity

A main reason to choose a quality audience to read your content is because quality lasts for the long-term, bad quality equals visitors that don't return to your blogging site. Yes, in the analytics sense, we look at the quality of visitors that attend your page each day too. Pay attention to this, because over time, knowing more about your audience will empower you as a blogger. Download Google Analytics and follow the instructions to see your blogs rank.

Know what kind of audience you are reaching. Gaining quality visits takes time, trust, loyalty, and somewhat of a platonic online friendship. If you want great visitors you have to treat your traffic great and provide them with quality, if you expect to get quality in return, you'd better dish it out. The universe gives what it gets.

Maintaining Your Blog

Maintaining your blog is a whole new story, now of course as we have been mentioning, this takes a lot of hard driven sweat! Driven sweat, meaning you will be spending most of your hours blogging. Think of it this way, your friends that work the normal nine to five, they will be begging you to hang out and socialize with them, meanwhile, if you leave your computer for one second, than other bloggers will in fact rise to the top first! Don't let peer pressure reel you in from achieving your well sought out blogging dreams and goals.

Blogging is an extremely competitive market, so the moment that you drift off task, the moment that you step away from your computer, and take your hands off of your computer, is the moment where all of your future slips away. Just kidding, as a blogger, learn how to balance your work/life schedule. Yes, blogging is competitive, this fact won't change, but tackle this feat, if you really want it, you can do it! If you want to become an extremely serious blogger than it should be in your best interest to always write, write, write, and publish! But remember to publish with style, quality, and intent. Otherwise all of your readers will think that you are utterly incompetent. Who wants to be known as the 'incompetent blogger'? Word will get around and perhaps you'll get page views, but let's get real, the page views won't be considered quality followers if you damage you bloggers reputation and site by publishing incoherent words with tons of editing mistakes, that is exactly what your page viewers will take away. Don't ruin yourself and always publish wisely.

Headlines Are Crucial!

Everyone knows that not one person in their right mind will click on a title headline if they have no clue what it is about. When writing your blogging post headlines, you need to make sure that you choose an attention-getter headline. You need to choose a headline that is relevant to your blog post. Now that we are mentioning headlines, we can now begin to explore headlines more in depth. In order to understand headlines in a more intricate sense, we need to venture out, and research trends. In case you are new to trends, let's talk about trends, it is actually easier to find trends than you think.

Thanks to the advanced and easily accessible internet, we can find trends on social media sites such as: Facebook, Twitter, Instagram, Google, you name it, if you begin to research trends on these sites, chances are you'll find the answer to your question in a matter of seconds, with a simple search titled 'trends'. Now if you want to go deeper, which you should want to, as knowledge is power, (if we have no clue about ways to enhance our blogs earnings, then really, what is the point?). Studying trends can be an interesting experience, because when you get deeper into the research, you will be able to see that there really is no pattern when it comes to trends in the making, trends happen because of various reasons. Usually popularity inside of a trend will hit hard and then die down rather rapidly, with a new trend arising shortly after. Keeping up with daily trends will continue to give you an edge as a blogger. Every single day, make sure to set a time aside so that way you can research and study past and current trends. If you can make your content relevant to the times in 2016 and so on, and provide a quality read, visitors will be flocking to your blog site. Also shares and likes will become the normalcy. It is important to implement this task on a daily basis, as trends go in and out. Research!

Edit, Edit, Edit

Blogging, the only reason we are going to consistently stuff this advice in this book, *Making Money from Blogging,* is because blogging is mainly about content and visuals. Readers and audience love entertainment. Entertainment is what keeps our human lives interesting. Editing our content will continue to show our readers that we are serious about our blog and that we are serious about considering our blog a business. The keywords that exemplify blogging are, professionalism, having an edge, and learning how to connect to an online community of people.

SEO Keywords, Utmost Importance

SEO content and keywords, what is this? Well, to make things simple, SEO stands for search engine optimization. We all should be aware that Google is not only a global player, but an extremely useful tool when it comes to online searching and content. Using Google and working in unison with Google, will ensure that your blogging website and business grows. Make sure to add SEO content into your blogging site, in other words, make sure that your content is density rich in keyword content, by at least 45-55%, if you want to eventually become visible online. An example, say your blog content is about medicine and the human spine, well, you'd better make sure that you decide on keywords and flood your content with the keywords that you choose, this will help your content be found online. In this case, you can use keywords such as: 'human spine' and 'medicine'.

WordPress

If you are a blogger, than it is wise that you know how to use WordPress, you need to be able to be technically savvy; otherwise the next blogger will be read and followed over you! Don't limit yourself, by not learning the proper technical skills and information that you need to learn to complete a professional looking blog. WordPress started in the year, 2003 as a C.M.S based company, a content management system. WordPress is used as a professional source to share content, utilize all of the blogging tools out there. We most certainly recommend signing up with wordpress.com.

Blogger

Blogger is another platform that is useful for all bloggers around. Keep in mind when blogging, it is never useful to only use one platform, publish, spread your content, link it, and connect it to your original site, if you really want to optimize the amount of viewers that you have and will soon gain. A little background information about Blogger, Blogger is actually connected to Google Adsense, remember this, we've mentioned it twice, so if you are immediately looking to monetize your blog earnings, than it is incredibly wise that you initially start with Blogger, since Blogger works hand and hand with Google Adsense.

Facebook

Facebook, ah Facebook, the glory of social media and connecting to one another. With Facebook we are now able to communicate on a grand and global level. Staying in touch across the globe has never been so easy. When you begin your blogging career, you also need to make sure that you publish, and you share your quality blog posts on your online social media site, Facebook. Otherwise, how will your peers and future readers know that you even exist? Don't just sit around and expect people to knock on your door, you gotta pound the pavement, and knock away at doors, yes, that is right, you are the blogger, you want to be read? So you have to be the knocker. Facebook is a great tool to market your blogging content to your friends and family. Let's say that you have one thousand friends on your friend list, your other friend has three thousand; technically speaking, if you convince your friend to share your latest blog post, your new market reach would now be four thousand people, and the numbers will continue to increase upon how many shares the blog post gets. Post, share, and like, these are pertinent in the world of online blogging. This step will ultimately lead you to monetary success; don't forget, the more money in your pocket, the sooner you are to your lavish retirement.

- **Rules to follow on Facebook:**
- First and foremost, realize that Facebook is much more of a personal site rather than Twitter, LinkedIn, etc. On Facebook, sure sometimes we have our work associates, but we also have our friends and family, make sure to post away

- Don't over post as you could irritate your readers
- Watch how the diction in your content is exerted
- Keep your tone warm and friendly

LinkedIn

No one really thinks about LinkedIn when it comes to blogging, but what some bloggers are missing out on is the ability to reach a bigger and bigger audience, you are darn right, our advice is to post your blogging links on LinkedIn. Of course every site has its own etiquette, so make sure you follow the proper etiquette when posting on any site, being aware of this factor, will only help you, before you make a detrimental posting mistake that likely causes you trouble or less traffic down the road. Okay, enough, onto positivity, what bloggers miss is that if you are a member of LinkedIn, you have the ability to follow and join certain groups, you can choose related niches to follow, simply by the stroke of a proper keyword search, which can then lead you to a plethora of an entire horizon of a whole new network! Post gracefully and wisely, yet remember, LinkedIn, is not like Twitter or Facebook, LinkedIn, is one of its own, and is a social platform site directed at connecting business professionals all around the world. So be sure to complete your profile and make sure that you provide one simple, clean, and professionally looking photo. Publish relevant blog information on LinkedIn occasionally, too much is never good, especially on LinkedIn.

Twitter

So many social media sites exist in the year 2016. Twitter offers another route for bloggers.

Twitter is different than Facebook as Twitter is known to be less personal and more for business alerts. Twitter allows a way for users to share information globally with a short amount of characters, (words). Say something concise and brief, yet get your point across is the entire feel. Twitter is a good way to share blog links, it is a great way to gain an audience of followers that you can eventually link back to your blog site, in turn gaining you quality visitors that actual visit your blog site because they actually get something in return from your site, whether it is advice or some kind of tangible item. If your visitors are receiving something great, they will be satiated. More traffic equals more money for the blogger. Add your blog website to your Twitter profile, anyone and everyone can now have access to your blog, so as long as you are okay with this fact, then everything should be green and ready to go.

Rules to follow on Twitter:

- Be concise
- Post relevancy only
- Don't over post
- Reblog other Twitter users
- Communicate in a friendly yet professional way with other users
- Be mindful of the words you post
- Add images as this will increase your chances of receiving more viewers/traffic
- You need to have killer headlines!! (Utmost important!)
- Like other posts, be sociable, and welcoming if you want more followers

- Keep in mind, more followers on Twitter, will mean more visibility for your ever so precious blog that you have created.

The Importance of Widgets

Have you ever been reading a blog and you loved it so much that you wanted to share this wonderful and new blog post, but sadly you were unable to because there were no share buttons? The share buttons or the reblog buttons were non-existent, which then limited you, preventing you from re blogging the great and fabulous Author whom you just discovered. Sadly the Author could have had many more followers once you reblogged the glorious piece of art. This particular Artist limited themselves, by not adding widgets onto their blog site. Always add social share widgets to each blog post! Why wouldn't you?

Hone Your Creativity

When we say hone your creativity what we really mean, is hustle your way to more cash flow! You need to tap into the creative you and you need to be able to create and think of various ways in which you can rake in more dough. You need to stretch your arms out to various paths. Choosing one path in the blogging world isn't all that smart. When we mention paths, we want you to start thinking more and more outside of the box as we've been mentioning. You need to be able to not only blog on your blogging website, but you need to get creative and start offering more things on your site that will lead to financial gain.

Let's talk more in depth about paths, we need to offer our visitors: eBooks, products, services, or advertising; this is where the mula really comes from. Say you are a financial consultant, not only can you sell financial services on your website blog, but you can jump outside of the box and start to create quality eBooks that offer financial consulting, your traffic will love this, if it is well written. Of course, create a strategy before you even begin to start. An example strategy would be, offering your visitors a free and valuable eBook for their pure enjoyment. Your blog visitors will love you for this mere gesture and they will surely come back to visit your site, but the next time they do, you as the blogger should upload your newly written eBook, this time charge for it. Chances are if your visitors loved your first free eBook, your teaser, chances are, they will take a chance, and buy your second book. The free giveaway strategy always makes visitors feel appreciated and of course people want to come back if they feel like someone is actually appreciating them and solving their problems at the same time. There are many ways to monetize a blog, so don't forget this fact.

Promotional giveaways also prove to help your service, product, or business, why? Well, the answer is easy, if you offer a limited amount of something to the public, and it is in fact a quality product or service, well then, word will travel, and reviews will flood in. Start thinking about giving back to people, before you start thinking about how you will rake in more cash. If you are too concentrated on the cash at hand, you will not be providing your visitors with ultimate results, as you will be too concerned on receiving than giving, this is never good. Do not fall into this trap when you become a blogger, otherwise risk losing visitors early on.

Strategize Your Marketing Efforts

If you are wanting to switch your nine to five mundane life schedule into a full blown online blogger then get ready to market your entire efforts away, day in and day out. Marketing isn't such a breezy process as it is an absolute time guzzler. The only way to market, is to consistently reach out and tell the world about your blog, product, service, giveaway, your brand, etc., you have to be vocal when it comes to communication and being a blogger. Marketing is important, not only is the actual process of marketing necessary, this is an ongoing and never ending implementation. Next up, is analyzation. Set-up a plan to know the numbers. Know viewer traffic numbers in order to assess and analyze trends on certain days, certain times, and years, etc. Learn about the demographic population that you are reaching. Ask yourself questions such as; what types of demographics do you want to reach? What age group? Region? All of these questions are helpful to know because if you study your viewers, chances are you will be able to solve their needs, rather than if you didn't know anything about them. How will you solve your viewer's needs? This is especially important. Once you know what your niche is, and once you have a good amount of posts that are of course, a hand crafted piece of quality nature, then you can begin your marketing endeavors. Although marketing endeavors go a long way, if sales numbers and financials are not coming in, then we can classify marketing efforts as ineffective and defective. Always strategize appropriately. Write down your blogger's business plan.

Analyzation Strategies

- **Google Analytics (suggested)**

Abilities include: Viewing demographic and region data, viewing the amount of visitors per day, including data regarding exact time, location, gender, age, etc.; this marketing data can be retrieved from an awesome platform provided from one of the top players in the IT sector, Google! Maximize the tools that have been freely handed to you. Google offers us great free tools, now utilize Google and Blogger. You may be asking yourself, what exactly will you be doing with the information that you are retrieving? You can simply use the data to improve your viewer's experience, that is one thing you can do as a blogger, you can also use this data, to make sure that you are hitting your target goals. Hitting your target goals, will ensure that you keep rising the ladder. Once you download Google Analytics and you are able to view your tangible traffic, you can then start to realize that *Making Money from Blogging* is actually possible.

Sales

Okay, so your marketing skills worked and you now have a few sales, whether it is from your posted eBook, a client emailed you to provide services for them, a visitor buys your product, or your film and video sell, whatever the sale, you need to be able to keep up with the sales department. Always keep in mind that marketing and sales go hand-in-hand. In order for anyone to know about what you do or what your intention is, they need to be impressed with the image and the brand, before looking further. Once you catch your visitors with intent, and a way to solve their problem, you can then reel them in with a quality and a unique type of voice. Before you start posting your products and or services, you as the blogger, need to tap into the entrepreneur side of your soul. Tapping into your business side, you need to start researching industry rates and pricing, decide on your pricing strategy before you begin, and stick to it. Don't limit yourself and accept rates that clearly are low ball rates, have dignity and patience, and seek for quality clients. Here is some great advice, you exert quality, well in a world full of karma, a boomerang of quality is bound to come back to the striving blogger, as long as pure determination is shown. Sales is a numbers game and can be very frustrating for some. Being a professional blogger, who actually makes money off of blogging doesn't just require content skills; this requires a vast amount of different skills, in order for the blogger to survive in the competitive world of blogging. Hone various skills.

Rinse and Repeat

    Blogging is an ongoing process, once you start, once you light a fire with your fuel (your blogging content), and once you gain a momentum with your daily, weekly, monthly, and yearly visitors you can't stop blogging, this is a process that must be rinsed and repeated with a non-stop attitude, day by day. Sound too grueling? Now is your chance to drop-out, but we are just giving the realistic facts here in the year 2016. Perhaps one day you will outgrow your blog, as you will have surpassed all of the goals that you set out for your blog to accomplish? At this point in your blogging career, you are making so much money from in, it pays for itself, all you do is post blogging content, and it pays. Perhaps you don't feel like posting every single day anymore, perhaps the years have passed and you are now in an authoritative stance and position. At this point, you can then use a strategy of using the profit earned, and pay other writers to write future content for you. Of course you need proper and qualified applicants; otherwise you risk poor blogging content. But don't worry as everything needs to be approved before being published, and approval must be granted by the CEO of course, and in this case, the CEO is now you. Choose quailed writers to help you out when it comes to writing your blogging content, this couldn't be such a bad idea. Qualified meaning, a rad portfolio with an accredited college degree, plus experience. Yes, you as a business owner will be paying a staff of writers to write quality blogging posts, but as long as the viewers continue to rake in, you are still making money. Make a point to bring in more profit than you are spending, this will surely keep you on a path built with financial security and success, *Making Money From Blogging* is real, it is actual and factual!

If you eventually work yourself up to this opportunity and position, then it is wise if you spend and keep track of your finances wisely, you will need a bookkeeper and an accountant at this point. Choose whether or not blogging is your path. Once you get to this point in your blogging career, you'll be able to choose whether or not you want to work remotely and control a staff of bloggers that you hire, while you are enjoying yourself traveling the entire globe. Or you can choose to simply relax and manage your team all from the comfort of your home near a creek. Mind you, once your blogging site prevails with millions of visitors each day, you will be able to pay off your entire mortgage in one shot, so keep at it. When you are a successful blogger, you can choose your destiny, you are no longer, what we consider, 'corporate capped'. You as a blogger and a freelance entrepreneur have an opportunity for limitless possibilities, these possibilities will allow you to make maximum profit. The sky really is the limit in this case, as the sales, and blogging efforts are all up to you, you are the boss, so tread with a fierce and competitive force in the blogging world. Speak loudly, have dignity, gain respect, and provide knowledge, solutions, and a helping hand, to your blogging community and all around. Your work and the effort you put into it doesn't represent a company or a corporation, the amount of work that you provide for your blog, your brand, will in turn reflect a large amount on you, the blog owner.

Staying In-The-Know

As stated, there is no set formula when it comes to blogging, but following the above advice will surely help any blogger get set and ready to head onto a journey of blogging. Blogging can be a hit or miss when it comes to choosing a proper domain title, realize when one of your sites clearly just doesn't work out, just let it go, bite the bullet, and just create another one. Once you love your niche to a point where you do not hate what you are doing, can you then begin to flourish as an actual blogger. Since there is really no particular formula to follow in the art of blogging, every successful blogger needs to be a cutthroat hustler, otherwise other bloggers will be preferred. This is a scary thought for every individual blogger; of course you want the attention to veer towards your blogging site, not the other blogger! In order to outdo your competition you need to constantly be reading, day and night, don't just concentrate on creating massive amounts of content. Your viewers don't want to be flooded, in fact they want to see miracles and beautiful posts, not sloppy junk that hits their screens and eventually makes them cringe. Don't be out of your mind! The annoying marketing strategy doesn't work when we are striving for quality.

If you have the opportunity and the means to do it, it would be wise to take design classes, as this skill can help you as a blogger learn important tools. Learn software such as: Photoshop, Illustrator, Adobe Suite, etc. knowing more, will place you in an advantageous spot in the online world. You don't need to spend an arm and a leg when it comes to taking these classes, but it would be beneficial for you, especially if you don't know the basics, of Photoshop or Illustrator. Viewers love graphics, and if you have original photography, your photo can always pop more if you edit it on a software such as, Illustrator or Photoshop. Popping and crisp looking images that satisfy the reader's eyes will prove more and more traffic over time. You'd better be advertising crisp images on your blog at this point, that is, if you are in fact receiving a lot of traffic, otherwise you could be cutting yourself short.

Things to remember:
- Continuously educate yourself
- Learn new systems and software as it emerges, this will only help you, the blogger

- Attend workshops and seminars, you don't necessary need a full-blown college degree to be a blogger, of course, we recommended college, as a Bachelor's degree rounds the mind and proves to help every individual look outside-of-the-box, especially in western nations.
- Read and research basically until your eyes fall out
- Keep these words at the surface of your brain, "you'll always be a student, learning your entire life, the world is vast, and the knowledge inside is infinite, learning is growth."
- We cannot stress this enough, quality over quantity posts only!

Keep Your Head Above Water, Know What to Do If Your Blog Is Not Succeeding

Of course, we are not telling you to quit your full-time job that pays your bills, especially if you have a family to care for and to feed. It is best that when any business owner starts any new business that they make sure they have funds stocked away in case there is an emergency that unfortunately arises. We always need to keep safety funds in our accounts. When you start a blog and you decide that you want to leave your nine to five job, you need to make sure that you have enough funds to tide you over for at least six months. The beginning is always the toughest period. We consider this the breakout period, which in this case, you want to be striving and performing at your maximum, so be like Nike and 'just do it'! Every blogger needs to build his or her audience. Content building and blogging is a process, a process that involves continuous tender love and care. But let's face the truth, if you really love what you do, and you chose a niche that interests you the most, plus you're making a regular and decent income, what do you have to complain about? Yes, nothing in life is perfect, this is true, but when it comes time for blogging, or better yet any endeavor that we set our hearts on, practice really does make perfect. Ongoing efforts and full devoted time will surely outdo competitors that are on their blogging game, 'every now and then'. A devoted blogger is a strong quality blogger, waiting to burst out into full succession, you'll get there.

If you need a part-time job while you build-up your audience, well then get one, there is no shame in working more hours, especially if you need a paycheck, don't acquire debt, you'll hold yourself back in life. Until blogging has proven to pay your bills and then some, can you then begin to call it a full-time job. If you are not making enough money, and can barely keep your head afloat, and you are drowning in bills, make the logical decision and get a part-time job while you begin to build you blogging empire. Blog every single day, converse, and send out those well-written proposals. Stay consistent, offer something to the universe and soon the universe will be bound to give back to you, the striving and helpful blogger.

Job Boards and Proposals

Luckily the internet is so vast, as this fact allows us to have unlimited opportunities when it comes to online knowledge and monetary gains. If you are a freelance blogger, you can find jobs on sites like ProBlogger.com, the jobs posted on this site offer opportunities for bloggers to find paid jobs that actually pay the blogger per post. Learn to write convincing proposals in order to reel new clients in. You'd better not have one minuscule mistake in your proposal content, otherwise you will risk looking like a complete fool, and you better believe you most likely will not receive a response, and if you receive any kind of response, chances are the job poster will correct you proposal mistakes. When it comes to spelling, grammar, and punctuation, you never want to throw off your reading audience simply by disrupting the flow.

Massacre's Regarding Blogger's, Current Events

Recently there has been reports of blogger's being attacked by extremist religious groups, these groups are threatening bloggers, and have even carried out actual killings among blogger's. Apparently extremist religious groups have carried out attacks and have justified their reasoning by saying the blogger was defaming an actual religion. Blogger's everywhere have a right to exercise freedom of speech, but as our internet grows, and cyber war continues, blogger's be alert. An American born blogger just recently has been hacked to death in Bangladesh, 2016. The motive? An extremist religious belief thought that the blogger was creating blasphemy, hence why they hacked him to death. Bangladesh has recently received media, stating that their country is changing due to an influx of extremist religious beliefs. The story is still evolving, to read more about this blogger tragedy, please see CNN.com for more information.[1] As we get deeper into the cyber war that we are currently in, in the year 2016, we as bloggers need to stand strong with our free thinking, freedom of speech ideologies, we should maintain to keep. But we also need to be more vigilant, as a cyber war has sprung, whether anyone wants to announce it or not. Be the change, and offer glorious and helpful information. Do not be the blogger that offers corrupt information, otherwise legal suits could rise, or inciting violence is also another occurrence that could take place.

---

[1] http://www.cnn.com/2016/06/20/asia/bangladesh-avijit-roy-suspect-killed/

Sure we should feel comfortable, being that our first amendment protects us as law abiding citizens with freedom of speech, but as we read this news story case, a free-thinker blogger who lived in a predominantly religious country, was hacked for speaking his mind? This resonates deeply with us, be careful how you write, but speak up, and speak enlightenment, as good shall always prevail. By no means, shall self-expression equal fatality. To have such an ideology is monstrous. Blogger's all around, try to write from all sides of the story; neutrality is rather appealing to readers, as you tend to keep a sense of mystery. And who does not like mystery? Not us. Blog on!

Never Give Up Blogging

If blogging is a passion of yours and you've never made any money off of blogging, then it is likely that you didn't want to make money off of blogging in the first place. But if you dig deeper and place yourself in an entrepreneur and business mind stance, you can then begin to see profits and revenue flowing in. And don't you dare forget, blogging is not about one sole website, you must connect many links, products, and offerings, to your site in order for traffic to increase and come back to your site. Help your readers trust your site, and soon they will purchase anything on your site. If your true heart is set on telling the world how you feel, well then we advise that you do so, if you want to be an advocate and a journalist, by all means, be one. But if you do in fact choose the journalistic approach through your blogging site, make sure that you report only truth, and cite appropriately or you could very well end up with a slapped wrist and a law suit in the waiting. The internet has changed the way in which we conduct business, there are many litigation cases that are currently open regarding blogger's and accusations of slander and defamation, so be careful what you say in the year 2016. Remember, in journalism, you should be reporting just the facts anyway, read the law, on journalism, simply with a quick search on Google. Here in the United States, we are protected with our first amendment freedom of speech, but report with intent, truth, and dignity.

Thank you for reading and best of luck to you and your blog!

Your Free Gift

>>Download Your Free Book Here!<<

Are you interested in how you can generate thousands of dollars monthly from publishing eBooks on Amazon? Then please download this FREE book **The Kindle Publishing Game.** This book will give you all of the powerful information you need to get started earning passive income every month by creating high quality eBooks!

>>Download Your Free Book Here!<<